THIS PLANNER BELONGS TO

_____

# HOME ORGANISER

I really hope this planner helps to make your life a little bit easier.

This planner includes;

- Daily cleaning / shopping to do checklist - Organise cleaning tasks by room or priority, the choice is yours.

- Monthly checklist for bigger tasks such as, defrosting the freezer or having an annual wardrobe clear out

Adjust And Achieve - Copyright Protected, All Rights Reserved
No part of this publication may be reproduced, stored, copied or shared by any means, electronic or physical, or used in any manner without the prior written consent of the publisher.

# CLEANING & SHOPPING LISTS

## Living Room

- Hoover ✓
- Carpet Freshener ✓
- Change Wax Melts ✓
- Tidy Coffee Table ✓
- Clean Sofa ✓

## Olivia's Bedroom

- Change Bedding ✓
- Put Toys Away ✓
- Hoover ✓
- Polish
- Clean Blinds
- Put Dirty Washing On

## Jack's Bedroom

- Clean Blinds ✓
- Change Light Bulb ✓
- Put Away Clothes ✓

## Shopping

- Milk
- Eggs
- Chicken Breasts
- Cereal
- Tea Bags
- Bread
- Cheese
- Juice

# CLEANING CHECKLIST

## JANUARY
- [ ]
- [ ]
- [ ]
- [ ]
- [ ]
- [ ]

## FEBRUARY
- [ ]
- [ ]
- [ ]
- [ ]
- [ ]
- [ ]

## MARCH
- [ ]
- [ ]
- [ ]
- [ ]
- [ ]
- [ ]

## APRIL
- [ ]
- [ ]
- [ ]
- [ ]
- [ ]
- [ ]

## MAY
- [ ]
- [ ]
- [ ]
- [ ]
- [ ]
- [ ]

## JUNE
- [ ]
- [ ]
- [ ]
- [ ]
- [ ]
- [ ]

# CLEANING CHECKLIST

## JULY
- [ ]
- [ ]
- [ ]
- [ ]
- [ ]
- [ ]
- [ ]

## AUGUST
- [ ]
- [ ]
- [ ]
- [ ]
- [ ]
- [ ]
- [ ]

## SEPTEMBER
- [ ]
- [ ]
- [ ]
- [ ]
- [ ]
- [ ]
- [ ]

## OCTOBER
- [ ]
- [ ]
- [ ]
- [ ]
- [ ]
- [ ]
- [ ]

## NOVEMBER
- [ ]
- [ ]
- [ ]
- [ ]
- [ ]
- [ ]
- [ ]

## DECEMBER
- [ ]
- [ ]
- [ ]
- [ ]
- [ ]
- [ ]
- [ ]

# CLEANING & SHOPPING LISTS

# CLEANING & SHOPPING LISTS

# CLEANING & SHOPPING LISTS

# CLEANING & SHOPPING LISTS

# CLEANING & SHOPPING LISTS

# CLEANING & SHOPPING LISTS

# CLEANING & SHOPPING LISTS

# CLEANING & SHOPPING LISTS

# CLEANING & SHOPPING LISTS

# CLEANING & SHOPPING LISTS

# CLEANING & SHOPPING LISTS

# CLEANING & SHOPPING LISTS

# CLEANING & SHOPPING LISTS

# CLEANING & SHOPPING LISTS

# CLEANING & SHOPPING LISTS

# CLEANING & SHOPPING LISTS

# CLEANING & SHOPPING LISTS

# CLEANING & SHOPPING LISTS

# CLEANING & SHOPPING LISTS

# CLEANING & SHOPPING LISTS

# CLEANING & SHOPPING LISTS

# CLEANING & SHOPPING LISTS

# CLEANING & SHOPPING LISTS

# CLEANING & SHOPPING LISTS

# CLEANING & SHOPPING LISTS

# CLEANING & SHOPPING LISTS

# CLEANING & SHOPPING LISTS

# CLEANING & SHOPPING LISTS

# CLEANING & SHOPPING LISTS

# CLEANING & SHOPPING LISTS

# CLEANING & SHOPPING LISTS

# CLEANING & SHOPPING LISTS

# CLEANING & SHOPPING LISTS

# CLEANING & SHOPPING LISTS

# CLEANING & SHOPPING LISTS

# CLEANING & SHOPPING LISTS

# CLEANING & SHOPPING LISTS

# CLEANING & SHOPPING LISTS

# CLEANING & SHOPPING LISTS

# CLEANING & SHOPPING LISTS

# CLEANING & SHOPPING LISTS

# CLEANING & SHOPPING LISTS

# CLEANING & SHOPPING LISTS

# CLEANING & SHOPPING LISTS

# CLEANING & SHOPPING LISTS

# CLEANING & SHOPPING LISTS

# CLEANING & SHOPPING LISTS

# CLEANING & SHOPPING LISTS

# CLEANING & SHOPPING LISTS

# CLEANING & SHOPPING LISTS

# CLEANING & SHOPPING LISTS

# CLEANING & SHOPPING LISTS

# CLEANING & SHOPPING LISTS

# CLEANING & SHOPPING LISTS

# CLEANING & SHOPPING LISTS

# CLEANING & SHOPPING LISTS

# CLEANING & SHOPPING LISTS

# CLEANING & SHOPPING LISTS

# CLEANING & SHOPPING LISTS

# CLEANING & SHOPPING LISTS

# CLEANING & SHOPPING LISTS

# CLEANING & SHOPPING LISTS

# CLEANING & SHOPPING LISTS

# CLEANING & SHOPPING LISTS

# CLEANING & SHOPPING LISTS

# CLEANING & SHOPPING LISTS

# CLEANING & SHOPPING LISTS

# CLEANING & SHOPPING LISTS

# CLEANING & SHOPPING LISTS

# CLEANING & SHOPPING LISTS

# CLEANING & SHOPPING LISTS

# CLEANING & SHOPPING LISTS

# CLEANING & SHOPPING LISTS

# CLEANING & SHOPPING LISTS

# CLEANING & SHOPPING LISTS

# CLEANING & SHOPPING LISTS

# CLEANING & SHOPPING LISTS

# CLEANING & SHOPPING LISTS

# CLEANING & SHOPPING LISTS

# CLEANING & SHOPPING LISTS

# CLEANING & SHOPPING LISTS

# CLEANING & SHOPPING LISTS

# CLEANING & SHOPPING LISTS

# CLEANING & SHOPPING LISTS

# CLEANING & SHOPPING LISTS

# CLEANING & SHOPPING LISTS

# CLEANING & SHOPPING LISTS

# CLEANING & SHOPPING LISTS

# CLEANING & SHOPPING LISTS

# CLEANING & SHOPPING LISTS

# CLEANING & SHOPPING LISTS

# CLEANING & SHOPPING LISTS

# CLEANING & SHOPPING LISTS

# CLEANING & SHOPPING LISTS

# CLEANING & SHOPPING LISTS

# CLEANING & SHOPPING LISTS

# CLEANING & SHOPPING LISTS

# CLEANING & SHOPPING LISTS

# CLEANING & SHOPPING LISTS

# CLEANING & SHOPPING LISTS

# CLEANING & SHOPPING LISTS

# CLEANING & SHOPPING LISTS

# CLEANING & SHOPPING LISTS

# CLEANING & SHOPPING LISTS

# CLEANING & SHOPPING LISTS

# CLEANING & SHOPPING LISTS

# CLEANING & SHOPPING LISTS

# CLEANING & SHOPPING LISTS

# CLEANING & SHOPPING LISTS

# CLEANING & SHOPPING LISTS

Printed in Great Britain
by Amazon